家計簿

KAKEIBO

THE JAPANESE ART OF SAVING MONEY

FUMIKO

PENGUIN BOOKS

UK | USA | Canada | Ireland | Australia
India | New Zealand | South Africa

Penguin Books is part of the Penguin Random House
group of companies whose addresses can be found
at global.penguinrandomhouse.com.

First published 2017

001

Copyright © Fumiko Chiba, 2017

The moral right of the author has been asserted

Design by Maru Studio
Proverb pages designed by Midori Yamanaka
Additional illustrations by ingectar-e

Printed in Italy by L.E.G.O. S.p.A

A CIP catalogue record for this book is available
from the British Library

ISBN: 978-1-405-93613-2

MIX
Paper from
responsible sources
FSC® C018179

Penguin Random House is committed to a
sustainable future for our business, our readers
and our planet. This book is made from Forest
Stewardship Council® certified paper.

Kakeibo
家計簿
[pronounced 'kah-keh-boh']

People in Japan are masters of minimal living, able to make do with less in all aspects of life, whether it's de-cluttering personal belongings or savvy seasonal cooking. But at the heart of all this is the *kakeibo*: the budgeting journal used to set saving goals and spend wisely.

The premise is simple: at the beginning of each month you sit down with your *kakeibo* and think mindfully about how much you would like to save and what you will need to do in order to reach your goal. The *kakeibo* then gives you space to jot down your weekly spending and reflect on the month just gone. The simple act of completing your *kakeibo* ensures that saving is a part of your everyday life, while also giving you the opportunity to improve every month.

By using this *kakeibo*, you can get a grip on your spending and start to achieve your goals, finding ways to save for the things that really matter in your life.

The *kakeibo* has been a Japanese tradition stretching back for over a century. It was first popularized in 1904 by Hani Motoko, Japan's first female journalist, as a way for housewives to manage budgets. Although Japan is a traditional culture in many ways, the *kakeibo* was a liberating tool for women, giving them control over all financial decisions.

Throughout the twentieth century, the Japanese government actively promoted the *kakeibo* in order to compete with Western economies. Japan relied on its households to be self-sufficient and the *kakeibo* was a crucial tool for enabling personal savings despite low incomes.

Today, the *kakeibo* remains hugely popular across Japan as a tried-and-tested method of saving money. There are many types of *kakeibo*, but they all share a means for tracking income and recording expenditure.

Unlike in the West, Japan is still very much a cash society and bank cards are not widely used. Many people in Japan use their *kakeibo* to carefully allocate their allowance for each category of spending, and then physically divide their cash into little envelopes to help keep within their limits.

With apps linked to our bank cards, it's never been easier to see where our money is going, but often this only shows us where we are going *wrong*. This *kakeibo* will help show you the bigger picture and allow you to plan your spending more wisely.

There is much that can be learnt from how the Japanese approach their personal finances, but to get you started, here are some top tips:

Saving money is about spending money _well_.
Often when we think about saving money, the emphasis is on what we _cannot_ spend. This makes saving money a chore and prevents us from making it a long-term lifestyle change. The key to saving is to instead start thinking about it in terms of spending money – but spending it _well_. This is very important for changing your focus.

Divide your spending into 'musts' and 'wants'.
This _kakeibo_ will ask you to note down your essential and fixed outgoings at the beginning of each month, but everything else that you track on a weekly basis is variable. Within this, it's important to recognize the difference between 'must haves' and 'want tos'. You need to eat, but eating at an expensive restaurant is a 'want to', not a 'must have' – there is a crucial difference! Keep a check on what proportion of your spending is a 'must have', and this is a quick way to identify areas of waste in your spending.

how it works

Your *kakeibo* will guide you easily through the process of saving money by asking you to reflect on four key questions every month:

1) How much money do you have available?
Calculate this by deducting any fixed expenditure (e.g. rent or travelcard) from your monthly take-home pay.

2) How much would you like to save?
Set yourself a saving target and use this to calculate weekly spending limit you will need in order to meet your savings goal.

3) How much are you spending?
Keep a journal of your spending by jotting down the daily totals of your expenditure next to categories of your choosing.

4) How can you improve?
Reflect on your progress at the end of each week and month to see if you're on track to meet your target. Think about what you would change for next month.

Completing your *kakeibo* will keep your savings target at the forefront of your mind, allowing you to achieve the goals you want painlessly.

This book isn't tied to any particular dates, so you can start it on any day of any month of any year.

The kakeibo cycle...

How much
money do you
have available?

How can
you improve?

How much
would you like
to save?

How much
are you spending?

how it works: **spending plan**

How much money do you have coming in?
List all sources of income and your take-home pay for each (i.e. after immediate deductions such as tax, insurance, pension, student loan, etc.)

How much money do you have going out?
Jot down your fixed monthly outgoings (i.e. not things that vary such as food).

this **month is** *October*

How much money do you have coming in?

DATE	SOURCE		AMOUNT
15th	salary	£	1500
22nd	freelance	£	200
		£	
		£	
		TOTAL (A) £	1700

How much money do you have going out?

DATE	CATEGORY	AMOUNT
15th	rent	£ 600
15th	electricity	£ 10
15th	gas	£ 10
15th	water	£ 10
20th	internet	£ 9
20th	phone	£ 16
25th	gym	£ 45
		£
		£
	TOTAL (B)	£ 700

How much money do you have available to you?

TOTAL (A)	-	TOTAL (B)	=	TOTAL (C)
£ 1700		£ 700		£1000

How much money do you have available to you?
Subtract the total in question 2 from the total in question 1 (i.e. your fixed outgoings from your income) to find the total amount available.

How much do you want to save?

Set yourself a figure for how much you would like to have saved by the end of the month. Be realistic – if you usually struggle to save £100 a month, you're unlikely to suddenly start saving £500 – and might feel deflated if you don't achieve this. However, as you progress with your kakeibo, you should become more ambitious, and stretch the amount you want to save each month.

How much do you want to save?

TOTAL (D)	£ 200

What for?

Christmas presents for the family

How much should you spend?

TOTAL (C)	−	TOTAL (D)	=	TOTAL (E) (PER MONTH)
£ 1000		£ 200		£ 800

TOTAL (E)	÷	N° OF WEEKS	=	TOTAL (PER WEEK)
£ 800		4		£ 200

NOTES

How much should you spend?

Subtract the amount you want to save (TOTAL D) from the amount you have available (TOTAL C) to get the remaining total. Then divide this by the number of weeks until your next payday to find a weekly figure.

NOTES

Add your goal for the month or some encouragements.

how it works: **weekly spending**

Fill in your weekly spending budget.

Add your own categories to fit your lifestyle. In the examples on the right, takeaway might include evening takeaway but also coffee takeaway and a sandwich at lunchtime. Entertainment might include cinema and books.

3

Fill in your spending as you go along.

4

Tally up the daily totals so you can check how much you spent every day.

Week One				weekly budget £
CATEGORY	/ MON.	/ TUE.	/ WED.	/ THU.
supermarket	18.34		11.35	
takeaway	2.75	4.99	2.50	2.50
eat-out				
newsp/mag.			6.00	
gifts				
clothing				
entertain.				
travel	2.50	2.50	2.50	2.50
TOTAL	£ 23.59	£ 7.49	£ 22.35	£ 5.00

/ FRI.	/ SAT.	/ SUN.		memo
		23.05	52.74	
2.75			15.49	
	12.00		12.00	
		3.00	9.00	Saturday was Susan birhtday's party
	15.00		15.00	
	24.99		24.99	
	20.80		20.80	
2.50	7.00		19.50	
£ 5.25	£ 79.79	£ 26.05	£ 169.52	

5

Keep track of categories' totals as a way of analysing where your money goes.

6

Add any notes to self.

7

Check you haven't exceeded your limit.

how it works: **spending review**

1 Write TOTAL C from your spending plan.

2 Write TOTAL E from your spending plan.

3 Add the total of each weeks' spending for this month.

4 Substract the figure in point 3 from the figure in point 1.

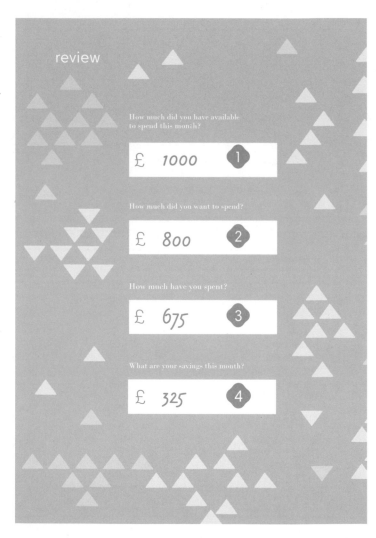

review

How much did you have available to spend this month?

£ 1000   **1**

How much did you want to spend?

£ 800   **2**

How much have you spent?

£ 675   **3**

What are your savings this month?

£ 325   **4**

This is the difference between TOTAL D in the spending plan versus what's actually left (point 4).

Did you meet your savings target this month?

Yes - I was aiming to save £200 and managed to save £325

Note down any ways you found to reduce your spending (e.g. preparing lunch at home rather than buying a sandwich at lunchtime).

What ways did you find to save money?

I started bringing a packed lunch to work

What areas did you spend too much on?

I spent quite a lot on clothes

By keeping tracks of the category totals week after week you can identify where your money goes.

What will you change next month?

I'll start planning evening meals in advance as well as lunch

Learn from this month and make plans for next month.

year planner

As you progress through this book, you will plan your spending on a month-by-month basis. But for now – take a deep breath and think about the year as a *whole*.

What special expenditure will occur during the course of the next twelve months?

Think about…

- Holidays: short breaks or longer trips

- Occasions: birthdays, weddings or Christmas

- Special events: a concert, festival or show

- Material goods: a new sofa or new phone

- Life events: moving house or embarking on a business venture

These things are all outside your usual daily or monthly outgoings, but by laying it out in this way you can see how frequent this 'once in a while' spending becomes.

Think about how much you would need to save each month to meet this total cost. Maybe this figure alone will be enough to stretch you, or maybe you could set yourself a more ambitious target. Either way, it's worth keeping this figure in mind to make sure that you are not caught short one month.

Once you've completed this table, you're ready to begin! Good luck, go for it, and just do your best. Or, as the Japanese say…

がんばって

GANBATTE!

MONTH	EVENT	AMOUNT
JANUARY		£
FEBRUARY		£
MARCH		£
APRIL		£
MAY		£
JUN		£
JULY		£
AUGUST		£
SEPTEMBER		£
OCTOBER		£
NOVEMBER		£
DECEMBER		£
	TOTAL	£

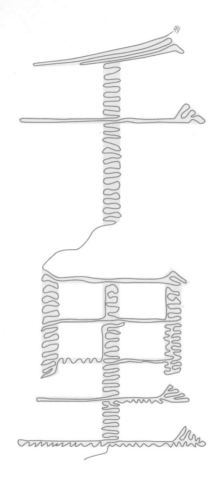

千里の道も一歩から

EVEN A THOUSAND-MILE JOURNEY BEGINS WITH THE FIRST STEP

This Japanese equivalent of Chinese philosopher Lao Tse's famous saying is a reminder that all journeys worth taking have to start somewhere.

month

1

this month is

How much money do you have coming in?

DATE	SOURCE	AMOUNT
		£
		£
		£
		£
	TOTAL (A)	**£**

How much money do you have going out?

DATE	CATEGORY	AMOUNT
		£
		£
		£
		£
		£
		£
		£
		£
		£
	TOTAL (B)	**£**

How much money do you have available to you?

TOTAL (A)	-	TOTAL (B)	=	TOTAL (C)
£		£		**£**

How much do you want to save?

TOTAL (D)	£

What for?

How much should you spend?

TOTAL (C)	-	TOTAL (D)	=	TOTAL (E) (PER MONTH)
£		£		£

TOTAL (E)	÷	N° OF WEEKS	=	TOTAL (PER WEEK)
£				£

NOTES

week one

weekly budget £

CATEGORY	/ MON.	/ TUE.	/ WED.	/ THU.
TOTAL	£	£	£	£

/ FRI.	/ SAT.	/ SUN.	TOTAL
£	£	£	£

memo

week two

weekly budget £

CATEGORY	/ MON.	/ TUE.	/ WED.	/ THU.
TOTAL	£	£	£	£

/ FRI.	/ SAT.	/ SUN.	TOTAL
£	£	£	£

memo

week three

weekly budget £

CATEGORY	/ MON.	/ TUE.	/ WED.	/ THU.
TOTAL	£	£	£	£

/ FRI.	/ SAT.	/ SUN.	TOTAL
£	£	£	£

memo

week four

weekly
budget £

CATEGORY	/	MON.	/	TUE.	/	WED.	/	THU.
TOTAL	£		£		£		£	

/ FRI.	/ SAT.	/ SUN.	TOTAL
£	£	£	£

memo

week five
(if needed this month)

weekly budget £

CATEGORY	/	MON.	/	TUE.	/	WED.	/	THU.
TOTAL	£		£		£		£	

/ FRI.	/ SAT.	/ SUN.	TOTAL
£	£	£	£

memo

review

How much did you have available
to spend this month?

£

How much did you want to spend?

£

How much have you spent?

£

What are your savings this month?

£

Did you meet your savings target this month?

What ways did you find to save money?

What areas did you spend too much on?

What will you change next month?

覆水盆に返らず

水水水盆
水水水水水水水

覆
水

覆
水

覆
水

覆
水

FUKUSUI BON NI KAERAZU

SPILLED WATER DOES NOT
RETURN TO THE TRAY

*Once it's spent, your money will not come back! Luckily
though, every month is the chance to start afresh, and attempt
to spill less water…*

month

2

this month is [   ]

How much money do you have coming in?

DATE	SOURCE	AMOUNT
		£
		£
		£
		£
	TOTAL (A)	**£**

How much money do you have going out?

DATE	CATEGORY	AMOUNT
		£
		£
		£
		£
		£
		£
		£
		£
		£
	TOTAL (B)	**£**

How much money do you have available to you?

TOTAL (A)	-	TOTAL (B)	=	TOTAL (C)
£		£		**£**

How much do you want to save?

TOTAL (D)	£

What for?

How much should you spend?

TOTAL (C)	-	TOTAL (D)	=	TOTAL (E) (PER MONTH)
£		£		£

TOTAL (E)	÷	N° OF WEEKS	=	TOTAL (PER WEEK)
£				£

NOTES

week one

weekly budget £

CATEGORY	/ MON.	/ TUE.	/ WED.	/ THU.
TOTAL	£	£	£	£

/ FRI.	/ SAT.	/ SUN.	TOTAL
£	£	£	£

memo

week two

weekly budget £

CATEGORY	/ MON.	/ TUE.	/ WED.	/ THU.
TOTAL	£	£	£	£

/ FRI.	/ SAT.	/ SUN.	TOTAL
£	£	£	£

memo

week three

weekly budget £ _____

CATEGORY	/ MON.	/ TUE.	/ WED.	/ THU.
TOTAL	£	£	£	£

/ FRI.	/ SAT.	/ SUN.	TOTAL
£	£	£	£

memo

week four

weekly budget £

CATEGORY	/	MON.	/	TUE.	/	WED.	/	THU.
TOTAL	£		£		£		£	

/ FRI.	/ SAT.	/ SUN.	TOTAL
£	£	£	£

memo

week five
(if needed this month)

weekly budget £ _____

CATEGORY	/	MON.	/	TUE.	/	WED.	/	THU.
TOTAL	£		£		£		£	

/ FRI.	/ SAT.	/ SUN.	TOTAL
£	£	£	£

memo

review

How much did you have available
to spend this month?

£

How much did you want to spend?

£

How much have you spent?

£

What are your savings this month?

£

Did you meet your savings target this month?

What ways did you find to save money?

What areas did you spend too much on?

What will you change next month?

猿も木から落ちる

SARU MO KI KARA OCHIRU

EVEN MONKEYS FALL FROM TREES

*If you found saving during these first months difficult,
don't be disheartened. We all make mistakes and
learning to tackle your finances takes practice.*

month
3

this month is [   ]

How much money do you have coming in?

DATE	SOURCE	AMOUNT
		£
		£
		£
		£
	TOTAL (A)	£

How much money do you have going out?

DATE	CATEGORY	AMOUNT
		£
		£
		£
		£
		£
		£
		£
		£
		£
	TOTAL (B)	£

How much money do you have available to you?

TOTAL (A)	-	TOTAL (B)	=	TOTAL (C)
£		£		£

How much do you want to save?

TOTAL (D)	£

What for?

How much should you spend?

TOTAL (C)	−	TOTAL (D)	=	TOTAL (E) (PER MONTH)
£		£		£

TOTAL (E)	÷	N° OF WEEKS	=	TOTAL (PER WEEK)
£				£

NOTES

week one

weekly budget £

CATEGORY	/ MON.	/ TUE.	/ WED.	/ THU.
TOTAL	£	£	£	£

/ FRI.	/ SAT.	/ SUN.	TOTAL
£	£	£	£

memo

week two

CATEGORY	/ MON.	/ TUE.	/ WED.	/ THU.
TOTAL	£	£	£	£

/ FRI.	/ SAT.	/ SUN.	TOTAL
£	£	£	£

memo

week three

CATEGORY	/ MON.	/ TUE.	/ WED.	/ THU.
TOTAL	£	£	£	£

/ FRI.	/ SAT.	/ SUN.	TOTAL
£	£	£	£

memo

week four

CATEGORY	/ MON.	/ TUE.	/ WED.	/ THU.
TOTAL	£	£	£	£

/ FRI.	/ SAT.	/ SUN.	TOTAL
£	£	£	£

memo

week five
(if needed this month)

weekly budget £ _____

CATEGORY	/ MON.	/ TUE.	/ WED.	/ THU.
TOTAL	£	£	£	£

/ FRI.	/ SAT.	/ SUN.	TOTAL
£	£	£	£

memo

review

How much did you have available
to spend this month?

£

How much did you want to spend?

£

How much have you spent?

£

What are your savings this month?

£

Did you meet your savings target this month?

What ways did you find to save money?

What areas did you spend too much on?

What will you change next month?

蟹は甲羅に似せて穴を掘る

KANI WA KŌRA NI NISETE ANA WO HORU

CRABS DIG HOLES ACCORDING TO THE SIZE OF THEIR SHELLS

Like the crab, we must behave proportionally to our means. Your income and aspirations to save should determine the extent of your spending.

month

this month is _____

How much money do you have coming in?

DATE	SOURCE	AMOUNT
		£
		£
		£
		£
	TOTAL (A)	**£**

How much money do you have going out?

DATE	CATEGORY	AMOUNT
		£
		£
		£
		£
		£
		£
		£
		£
		£
	TOTAL (B)	**£**

How much money do you have available to you?

TOTAL (A)	-	TOTAL (B)	=	TOTAL (C)
£		£		**£**

How much do you want to save?

TOTAL (D)	£

What for?

How much should you spend?

TOTAL (C)	-	TOTAL (D)	=	TOTAL (E) (PER MONTH)
£		£		£

TOTAL (E)	÷	N° OF WEEKS	=	TOTAL (PER WEEK)
£				£

NOTES

week one

weekly budget £

CATEGORY	/	MON.	/	TUE.	/	WED.	/	THU.
TOTAL	£		£		£		£	

/ FRI.	/ SAT.	/ SUN.	TOTAL
£	£	£	£

memo

week two

weekly budget £ _____

CATEGORY	/ MON.	/ TUE.	/ WED.	/ THU.
TOTAL	£	£	£	£

/ FRI.	/ SAT.	/ SUN.	TOTAL	memo
£	£	£	£	

week three

weekly budget £

CATEGORY	/ MON.	/ TUE.	/ WED.	/ THU.
TOTAL	£	£	£	£

/ FRI.	/ SAT.	/ SUN.	TOTAL
£	£	£	£

memo

week four

weekly budget £

CATEGORY	/ MON.	/ TUE.	/ WED.	/ THU.
TOTAL	£	£	£	£

/ FRI.	/ SAT.	/ SUN.	TOTAL
£	£	£	£

memo

week five
(if needed this month)

weekly budget £

CATEGORY	/ MON.	/ TUE.	/ WED.	/ THU.
TOTAL	£	£	£	£

/ FRI.	/ SAT.	/ SUN.	TOTAL
£	£	£	£

memo

review

How much did you have available
to spend this month?

£

How much did you want to spend?

£

How much have you spent?

£

What are your savings this month?

£

Did you meet your savings target this month?

What ways did you find to save money?

What areas did you spend too much on?

What will you change next month?

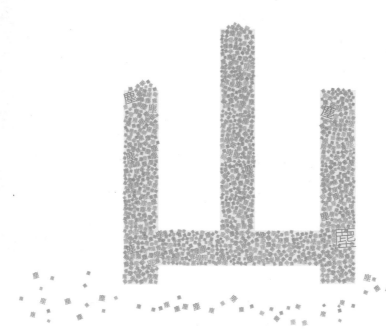

塵も積もれば山となる

CHIRI MO TSUMOREBA YAMA TO NARU

EVEN DUST AMASSED WILL
GROW INTO A MOUNTAIN

*This saying applies both to spending and saving! Think about
the little things you could give up or find cheaper alternatives
for, and imagine the mountain of savings you can achieve
by the end of the year.*

month

5

this month is [ ]

How much money do you have coming in?

DATE	SOURCE	AMOUNT
		£
		£
		£
		£
		TOTAL (A) £

How much money do you have going out?

DATE	CATEGORY	AMOUNT
		£
		£
		£
		£
		£
		£
		£
		£
		£
		TOTAL (B) £

How much money do you have available to you?

TOTAL (A)	-	TOTAL (B)	=	TOTAL (C)
£		£		**£**

How much do you want to save?

TOTAL (D)	£

What for?

How much should you spend?

TOTAL (C)	−	TOTAL (D)	=	TOTAL (E) (PER MONTH)
£		£		£

TOTAL (E)	÷	N° OF WEEKS	=	TOTAL (PER WEEK)
£				£

NOTES

week one

weekly budget £ _____

CATEGORY	/ MON.	/ TUE.	/ WED.	/ THU.
TOTAL	£	£	£	£

/ FRI.	/ SAT.	/ SUN.	TOTAL	memo
£	£	£	£	

week two

weekly budget £

CATEGORY	/ MON.	/ TUE.	/ WED.	/ THU.
TOTAL	£	£	£	£

/ FRI.	/ SAT.	/ SUN.	TOTAL
£	£	£	£

memo

week three

weekly budget £

CATEGORY	/ MON.	/ TUE.	/ WED.	/ THU.
TOTAL	£	£	£	£

/ FRI.	/ SAT.	/ SUN.	TOTAL	memo
£	£	£	£	

week four

weekly
budget £

CATEGORY	/ MON.	/ TUE.	/ WED.	/ THU.
TOTAL	£	£	£	£

/ FRI.	/ SAT.	/ SUN.	TOTAL	memo
£	£	£	£	

week five
(if needed this month)

weekly budget £

CATEGORY	/	MON.	/	TUE.	/	WED.	/	THU.
TOTAL	£		£		£		£	

/ FRI.	/ SAT.	/ SUN.	TOTAL	memo
£	£	£	£	

review

How much did you have available
to spend this month?

£

How much did you want to spend?

£

How much have you spent?

£

What are your savings this month?

£

Did you meet your savings target this month?

What ways did you find to save money?

What areas did you spend too much on?

What will you change next month?

身から出た錆

MI KARA DETA SABI

RUST COMES FROM WITHIN THE BODY

*Only we are ultimately responsible for our own bad habits.
If you have not yet found a pattern of sensible spending and
saving, you must look within yourself to find the motivation
and willingness to change.*

month

6

this month is [   ]

How much money do you have coming in?

DATE	SOURCE	AMOUNT
		£
		£
		£
		£
	TOTAL (A)	**£**

How much money do you have going out?

DATE	CATEGORY	AMOUNT
		£
		£
		£
		£
		£
		£
		£
		£
		£
	TOTAL (B)	**£**

How much money do you have available to you?

TOTAL (A)	-	TOTAL (B)	=	TOTAL (C)
£		£		**£**

How much do you want to save?

TOTAL (D)	£

What for?

How much should you spend?

TOTAL (C)	-	TOTAL (D)	=	TOTAL (E) (PER MONTH)
£		£		£

TOTAL (E)	÷	N° OF WEEKS	=	TOTAL (PER WEEK)
£				£

NOTES

week one

CATEGORY	/ MON.	/ TUE.	/ WED.	/ THU.
TOTAL	£	£	£	£

/ FRI.	/ SAT.	/ SUN.	TOTAL
£	£	£	£

memo

week two

budget £

CATEGORY	/ MON.	/ TUE.	/ WED.	/ THU.
TOTAL	£	£	£	£

/ FRI.	/ SAT.	/ SUN.	TOTAL	memo
£	£	£	£	

week three

CATEGORY	/	MON.	/	TUE.	/	WED.	/	THU.
TOTAL	£		£		£		£	

/ FRI.	/ SAT.	/ SUN.	TOTAL
£	£	£	£

memo

week four

CATEGORY	/	MON.	/	TUE.	/	WED.	/	THU.
TOTAL	£		£		£		£	

/ FRI.	/ SAT.	/ SUN.	TOTAL
£	£	£	£

memo

week five
(if needed this month)

CATEGORY	/	MON.	/	TUE.	/	WED.	/	THU.
TOTAL	£		£		£		£	

/ FRI.	/ SAT.	/ SUN.	TOTAL
£	£	£	£

memo

review

How much did you have available
to spend this month?

£

How much did you want to spend?

£

How much have you spent?

£

What are your savings this month?

£

Did you meet your savings target this month?

What ways did you find to save money?

What areas did you spend too much on?

What will you change next month?

七転び八起き

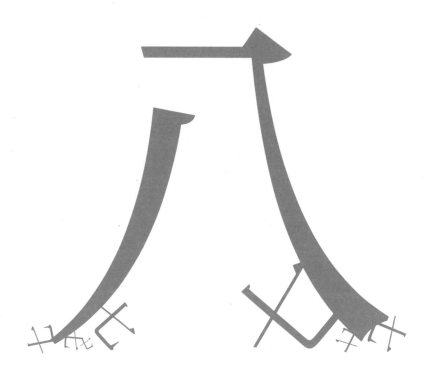

NANA KOROBI YA OKI

FALL DOWN SEVEN TIMES,
GET UP EIGHT

You are seven months into your kakeibo, *and hopefully haven't
fallen down seven times! But no matter how many times you
fail, your determination will lift you up again.*

month

7

this month is

How much money do you have coming in?

DATE	SOURCE	AMOUNT
		£
		£
		£
		£
	TOTAL (A)	**£**

How much money do you have going out?

DATE	CATEGORY	AMOUNT
		£
		£
		£
		£
		£
		£
		£
		£
		£
	TOTAL (B)	**£**

How much money do you have available to you?

TOTAL (A)	-	TOTAL (B)	=	TOTAL (C)
£		£		£

How much do you want to save?

TOTAL (D)	£

What for?

How much should you spend?

TOTAL (C)	-	TOTAL (D)	=	TOTAL (E) (PER MONTH)
£		£		£

TOTAL (E)	÷	N° OF WEEKS	=	TOTAL (PER WEEK)
£				£

NOTES

week one

weekly budget £

CATEGORY	/ MON.	/ TUE.	/ WED.	/ THU.
TOTAL	£	£	£	£

/ FRI.	/ SAT.	/ SUN.	TOTAL	memo
£	£	£	£	

week two

weekly budget £

CATEGORY	/ MON.	/ TUE.	/ WED.	/ THU.
TOTAL	£	£	£	£

/ FRI.	/ SAT.	/ SUN.	TOTAL
£	£	£	£

memo

week three

weekly budget £

CATEGORY	/ MON.	/ TUE.	/ WED.	/ THU.
TOTAL	£	£	£	£

/ FRI.	/ SAT.	/ SUN.	TOTAL
£	£	£	£

memo

week four

 weekly budget £

CATEGORY	/ MON.	/ TUE.	/ WED.	/ THU.
TOTAL	£	£	£	£

/ FRI.	/ SAT.	/ SUN.	TOTAL
£	£	£	£

memo

week five
(if needed this month)

weekly budget £

CATEGORY	/ MON.	/ TUE.	/ WED.	/ THU.
TOTAL	£	£	£	£

/ FRI.	/ SAT.	/ SUN.	TOTAL	memo
£	£	£	£	

review

How much did you have available
to spend this month?

£

How much did you want to spend?

£

How much have you spent?

£

What are your savings this month?

£

Did you meet your savings target this month?

What ways did you find to save money?

What areas did you spend too much on?

What will you change next month?

八十の手習い

HACHIJŪ NO TENARAI

ONE MAY STUDY
CALLIGRAPHY AT EIGHTY

If the Japanese can learn new skills well beyond the age of retirement, then it's never too late to learn how to manage your finances!

month

8

this month is ▮▮▮▮▮▮▮▮

How much money do you have coming in?

DATE	SOURCE	AMOUNT
		£
		£
		£
		£
	TOTAL (A)	**£**

How much money do you have going out?

DATE	CATEGORY	AMOUNT
		£
		£
		£
		£
		£
		£
		£
		£
		£
	TOTAL (B)	**£**

How much money do you have available to you?

TOTAL (A)	-	TOTAL (B)	=	TOTAL (C)
£		£		**£**

How much do you want to save?

TOTAL (D)	£

What for?

How much should you spend?

TOTAL (C)	-	TOTAL (D)	=	TOTAL (E) (PER MONTH)
£		£		£

TOTAL (E)	÷	N° OF WEEKS	=	TOTAL (PER WEEK)
£				£

NOTES

week one

weekly budget £

CATEGORY	/ MON.	/ TUE.	/ WED.	/ THU.
TOTAL	£	£	£	£

/ FRI.	/ SAT.	/ SUN.	TOTAL
£	£	£	£

memo

week two

CATEGORY	/ MON.	/ TUE.	/ WED.	/ THU.
TOTAL	£	£	£	£

/ FRI.	/ SAT.	/ SUN.	TOTAL
£	£	£	£

memo

week three

weekly budget £

CATEGORY	/ MON.	/ TUE.	/ WED.	/ THU.
TOTAL	£	£	£	£

/ FRI.	/ SAT.	/ SUN.	TOTAL
£	£	£	£

memo

week four

CATEGORY	/ MON.	/ TUE.	/ WED.	/ THU.
TOTAL	£	£	£	£

/ FRI.	/ SAT.	/ SUN.	TOTAL
£	£	£	£

memo

week five
(if needed this month)

weekly budget £

CATEGORY	/ MON.	/ TUE.	/ WED.	/ THU.
TOTAL	£	£	£	£

/ FRI.	/ SAT.	/ SUN.	TOTAL
£	£	£	£

memo

review

How much did you have available
to spend this month?

£

How much did you want to spend?

£

How much have you spent?

£

What are your savings this month?

£

Did you meet your savings target this month?

What ways did you find to save money?

What areas did you spend too much on?

What will you change next month?

膝とも談合

HIZA TOMO DANGŌ

CONSULT ANYONE,
EVEN YOUR KNEES

*Friends and family can provide an insight into the areas
where your spending habits are failing you. Ask them
for honest feedback – what could you do differently?
And what tips do they have for living more frugally?*

month

9

this month is ▢

How much money do you have coming in?

DATE	SOURCE	AMOUNT
		£
		£
		£
		£
	TOTAL (A)	£

How much money do you have going out?

DATE	CATEGORY	AMOUNT
		£
		£
		£
		£
		£
		£
		£
		£
		£
	TOTAL (B)	£

How much money do you have available to you?

TOTAL (A)	-	TOTAL (B)	=	TOTAL (C)
£		£		£

How much do you want to save?

TOTAL (D)	£

What for?

How much should you spend?

TOTAL (C)	-	TOTAL (D)	=	TOTAL (E) (PER MONTH)
£		£		£

TOTAL (E)	÷	N° OF WEEKS	=	TOTAL (PER WEEK)
£				£

NOTES

week one

CATEGORY	/ MON.	/ TUE.	/ WED.	/ THU.
TOTAL	£	£	£	£

/ FRI.	/ SAT.	/ SUN.	TOTAL
£	£	£	£

memo

week two

CATEGORY	/ MON.	/ TUE.	/ WED.	/ THU.
TOTAL	£	£	£	£

/ FRI.	/ SAT.	/ SUN.	TOTAL	memo
£	£	£	£	

week three

CATEGORY	/ MON.	/ TUE.	/ WED.	/ THU.
TOTAL	£	£	£	£

/ FRI.	/ SAT.	/ SUN.	TOTAL
£	£	£	£

memo

week four

CATEGORY	/ MON.	/ TUE.	/ WED.	/ THU.
TOTAL	£	£	£	£

/ FRI.	/ SAT.	/ SUN.	TOTAL	memo
£	£	£	£	

week five
(if needed this month)

weekly budget £

CATEGORY	/ MON.	/ TUE.	/ WED.	/ THU.
TOTAL	£	£	£	£

/ FRI.	/ SAT.	/ SUN.	TOTAL	memo
£	£	£	£	

review

How much did you have available
to spend this month?

£

How much did you want to spend?

£

How much have you spent?

£

What are your savings this month?

£

Did you meet your savings target this month?

What ways did you find to save money?

What areas did you spend too much on?

What will you change next month?

失敗は成功の母親

FAILURE IS THE
MOTHER OF SUCCESS

As you fill in your kakeibo, you will find some months more successful than others. But if you fail one month, you will learn something from it, and can use this to create success in the future.

month

10

this month is ▮▮▮▮▮▮

How much money do you have coming in?

DATE	SOURCE	AMOUNT
		£
		£
		£
		£
	TOTAL (A)	£

How much money do you have going out?

DATE	CATEGORY	AMOUNT
		£
		£
		£
		£
		£
		£
		£
		£
		£
	TOTAL (B)	£

How much money do you have available to you?

TOTAL (A)	-	TOTAL (B)	=	TOTAL (C)
£		£		£

How much do you want to save?

TOTAL (D)	£

What for?

....
....
....

How much should you spend?

TOTAL (C)	−	TOTAL (D)	=	TOTAL (E) (PER MONTH)
£		£		£

TOTAL (E)	÷	N° OF WEEKS	=	TOTAL (PER WEEK)
£				£

NOTES

week one

weekly budget £

CATEGORY	/ MON.	/ TUE.	/ WED.	/ THU.
TOTAL	£	£	£	£

/ FRI.	/ SAT.	/ SUN.	TOTAL		memo
£	£	£	£		

week two

weekly budget £

CATEGORY	/ MON.	/ TUE.	/ WED.	/ THU.
TOTAL	£	£	£	£

/ FRI.	/ SAT.	/ SUN.	TOTAL
£	£	£	£

memo

week three

weekly budget £ _____

CATEGORY	/ MON.	/ TUE.	/ WED.	/ THU.
TOTAL	£	£	£	£

/ FRI.	/ SAT.	/ SUN.	TOTAL	*memo*
£	£	£	£	

week four

CATEGORY	/ MON.	/ TUE.	/ WED.	/ THU.
TOTAL	£	£	£	£

/ FRI.	/ SAT.	/ SUN.	TOTAL
£	£	£	£

memo

week five
(if needed this month)

weekly budget £

CATEGORY	/ MON.	/ TUE.	/ WED.	/ THU.
TOTAL	£	£	£	£

/ FRI.	/ SAT.	/ SUN.	TOTAL	*memo*
£	£	£	£	

review

How much did you have available
to spend this month?

£

How much did you want to spend?

£

How much have you spent?

£

What are your savings this month?

£

Did you meet your savings target this month?

What ways did you find to save money?

What areas did you spend too much on?

What will you change next month?

雨だれ石を穿つ

石

AMADARE ISHI O UGATSU

RAINDROPS WILL WEAR
THROUGH A STONE

Just as small expenditure will eat through your pocket!

month
11

this month is [   ]

How much money do you have coming in?

DATE	SOURCE	AMOUNT
		£
		£
		£
		£
	TOTAL (A)	£

How much money do you have going out?

DATE	CATEGORY	AMOUNT
		£
		£
		£
		£
		£
		£
		£
		£
		£
	TOTAL (B)	£

How much money do you have available to you?

TOTAL (A)	-	TOTAL (B)	=	TOTAL (C)
£		£		£

How much do you want to save?

TOTAL (D)	£

What for?

How much should you spend?

TOTAL (C)	-	TOTAL (D)	=	TOTAL (E) (PER MONTH)
£		£		£

TOTAL (E)	÷	N° OF WEEKS	=	TOTAL (PER WEEK)
£				£

NOTES

week one

CATEGORY	/ MON.	/ TUE.	/ WED.	/ THU.
TOTAL	£	£	£	£

/ FRI.	/ SAT.	/ SUN.	TOTAL
£	£	£	£

memo

week two

CATEGORY	/ MON.	/ TUE.	/ WED.	/ THU.
TOTAL	£	£	£	£

/ FRI.	/ SAT.	/ SUN.	TOTAL
£	£	£	£

memo

week three

CATEGORY	/ MON.	/ TUE.	/ WED.	/ THU.
TOTAL	£	£	£	£

/ FRI.	/ SAT.	/ SUN.	TOTAL	memo
£	£	£	£	

week four

weekly budget £ _____

CATEGORY	/ MON.	/ TUE.	/ WED.	/ THU.
TOTAL	£	£	£	£

/ FRI.	/ SAT.	/ SUN.	TOTAL
£	£	£	£

memo

week five
(if needed this month)

weekly budget £ _____

CATEGORY	/ MON.	/ TUE.	/ WED.	/ THU.
TOTAL	£	£	£	£

/ FRI.	/ SAT.	/ SUN.	TOTAL	memo
£	£	£	£	

review

How much did you have available
to spend this month?

£

How much did you want to spend?

£

How much have you spent?

£

What are your savings this month?

£

Did you meet your savings target this month?

What ways did you find to save money?

What areas did you spend too much on?

What will you change next month?

折れるより曲がれ

ORERU YORI MAGARE

BETTER TO BOW
THAN TO BREAK

Hiding from your finances until you have none left pushes
you to breaking point, but gently modifying your
spending allows you to live within your means.

month
12

this month is

How much money do you have coming in?

DATE	SOURCE		AMOUNT
			£
			£
			£
			£
		TOTAL (A)	**£**

How much money do you have going out?

DATE	CATEGORY		AMOUNT
			£
			£
			£
			£
			£
			£
			£
			£
			£
		TOTAL (B)	**£**

How much money do you have available to you?

TOTAL (A)	-	TOTAL (B)	=	TOTAL (C)
£		£		**£**

How much do you want to save?

TOTAL (D)	£

What for?

How much should you spend?

TOTAL (C)	–	TOTAL (D)	=	TOTAL (E) (PER MONTH)
£		£		£

TOTAL (E)	÷	N° OF WEEKS	=	TOTAL (PER WEEK)
£				£

NOTES

week one

weekly budget £

CATEGORY	/ MON.	/ TUE.	/ WED.	/ THU.
TOTAL	£	£	£	£

/ FRI.	/ SAT.	/ SUN.	TOTAL
£	£	£	£

memo

week two

weekly budget £

CATEGORY	/ MON.	/ TUE.	/ WED.	/ THU.
TOTAL	£	£	£	£

/ FRI.	/ SAT.	/ SUN.	TOTAL
£	£	£	£

memo

week three

CATEGORY	/ MON.	/ TUE.	/ WED.	/ THU.
TOTAL	£	£	£	£

/ FRI.	/ SAT.	/ SUN.	TOTAL
£	£	£	£

memo

week four

weekly budget £

CATEGORY	/	MON.	/	TUE.	/	WED.	/	THU.
TOTAL	£		£		£		£	

/ FRI.	/ SAT.	/ SUN.	TOTAL	memo
£	£	£	£	

week five
(if needed this month)

weekly budget £

CATEGORY	/ MON.	/ TUE.	/ WED.	/ THU.
TOTAL	£	£	£	£

/ FRI.	/ SAT.	/ SUN.	TOTAL
£	£	£	£

memo

review

How much did you have available
to spend this month?

£

How much did you want to spend?

£

How much have you spent?

£

What are your savings this month?

£

Did you meet your savings target this month?

What ways did you find to save money?

What areas did you spend too much on?

What will you change next month?

acknowledgements

This book has been compiled by writer Fumiko Chiba, with the assistance of Japanese *kakeibo* experts, savings bloggers, financial journalists and *kakeibo* devotees. The author and publisher would particularly like to thank the following people:

Sophie Yamamoto for creating such a beautifully designed book

Midori Yamanake for her creative interpretations of the proverbs

Yukinobu Kitamura for his fascinating insight into the importance of *kakeibo* in Japan's socioeconomic history

Aki (author of *Aki's Easy Kakeibo***)** for her brilliantly useful tips on saving

Yukiko Ayres for her inspiring thoughts on what *kakeibo* means to her

Yuki Wada for her advice on how to make the most from your *kakeibo*

Akemi Solloway for her insight into *kakeibo*'s place in Japanese culture

Thanks also to **Annie Underwood, Beatrix McIntyre, Annabel Wilson, Nicolas Obregon, Minami Funakoshi** and **The Japan Society**